GUIDE TO

COSTA RICA

MARION MORRISON

Consultant: Marilyn E. de Sauter

Highlights for Children

CONTENTS

On the cover: Tropical rain forests cover much of the mainland and islands of *Golfo Dulce*, the Sweet Gulf, in the southern part of Costa Rica. The waters of the gulf are ideal for swimming and scuba-diving.

The publisher is grateful for the guidance of the Costa Rica Tourist Office in London and **Marilyn Echeverría de Sauter** of San José, Costa Rica. She has published ten children's books, which are used in many schools throughout Costa Rica. She uses her pen name, Lara Ríos. One of her novels, *Mo*, is included in the International Board on Books for Young People (IBBY) Honor List. She is currently president of the Children's Literature Institute, IBBY, Costa Rica.

Published by Highlights for Children
© 2000 Highlights for Children, Inc.
P.O. Box 18201
Columbus, Ohio 43218-0201
For information on *Top Secret Adventures*, visit www.tsadventures.com or call 1-800-962-3661.

10 9 8 7 6 5 4 3
ISBN 0-87534-572-7

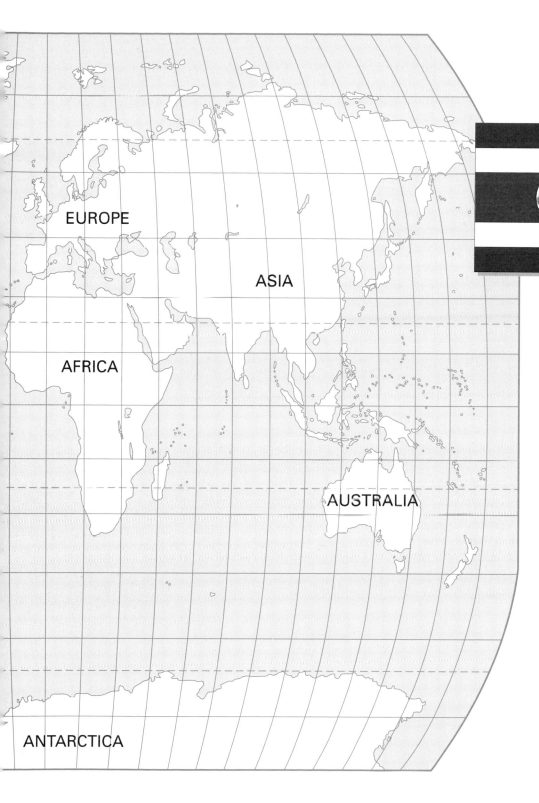

EUROPE

ASIA

AFRICA

AUSTRALIA

ANTARCTICA

△ **Costa Rica's Flag**
The flag shown here is the National Pavilion, used only for official acts. Another flag, without the coat of arms, is used more commonly. The blue, white, and red stripes represent the color of the sky, peace, and the blood of the country's heroes.

COSTA RICA AT A GLANCE

Area 19,730 square miles
(51,100 km^2)
Population 3,700,000
Capital San José, population of the
city and surroundings 1,200,000
Other big cities Alajuela (150,000),
San Isidro (110,000), Puerto
Limón (80,000)
Highest mountain Chirripó
Grande, 12,530 feet (3,819 m)
Longest river Rio Grande de
Térraba, 82 miles (131 km)
Largest lake Lake Arenal
Official language Spanish

▽ **Costa Rican stamps** The designs below show tropical rain forest plants and Christopher Columbus's three ships. Two designs honor Costa Rica's postal service and the international success of the country's soccer team.

◁**Costa Rican money** Costa Rica's currency is the colón. One colón is 100 céntimos. On the front of the 5-colón note is former President Rafael Castro. On the back of the note is a traditional scene, showing trade in coffee and bananas.

4

COSTA RICA

Lake Nicaragua

NICARAGUA

Caribbean Sea

Bahía de Santa Elena
La Cruz
Los Chiles
Santa Rita
Cordillera de Guanacaste
Miravalles
Frío
San Juan
Colorado
Golfo de Papagayo
Liberia
Bagaces
Lake Arenal
San Carlos
Puerto Viejo
Chirripó
Colorado
Sardinal
Cabo Velas
Filadelfia
Cañas
San Miguel
Parismina
TORTUGUERO NATIONAL PARK
Santa Cruz
Tempisque
Poás
Guápiles
Siquirres
Puerto Jesús
San Ramón
Barva
Nicoya
Alajuela
Heredia
Irazú
Puerto Limón
Península de Nicoya
Puntarenas
SAN JOSÉ
Guadalupe
10°N
Golfo de Nicoya
San Mateo
Río Grande de Térraba
Turrialba
Cartago
Punta Cahuita
Paquera
Suretka
Chirripó
Teliré
Cabo Blanco
Parrita
Cordillera de Talamanca
Puerto Quepos
San Isidro
Durika
Dominical
Buenos Aires
PACIFIC
Potrero Grande
OCEAN
Ciudad Cortés
Gran de Térraba
PANAMA
Palmar Sur
Bahía de Coronado
Punta San Pedrillo
Golfito
Península de Osa
Golfo Dulce

N
W E
S

Punta Burica
8°N

COSTA RICA

Farmland & Woodland
Mountains

★ Capital
● Major Cities
▲ Mountain Peaks
— Country Boundary

0   10   20 Miles
0 10 20 30 Kilometers

5

WELCOME TO COSTA RICA

Costa Rica is one of seven countries that make up Central America. Central America is an isthmus (bridge of land) that connects the continents of North and South America. To the north of Costa Rica lies Nicaragua and to the south is Panama. To the east lies the Caribbean Sea, and the Pacific Ocean is on the west. The western coastline is longer because of the many bays and peninsulas.

Hot, humid lowlands lie along the coasts, but much of Costa Rica's interior is mountainous. Four main *cordilleras,* or mountain ranges, cross the country, and there are volcanoes that cause earthquakes.

Most of the people live in the highlands where the capital, San José, is located. The city lies in the center of the country's agricultural heartland. Most of the coffee, for which Costa Rica is well known, grows here. Large plantations of bananas, Costa Rica's other major crop, are located in the tropical coastal lowlands.

▽ **Deadly poisonous frogs** These tiny, colorful frogs of the rain forest are poison-arrow frogs. Glands in their skin produce a poison so deadly that it was once used by some Native Americans on their hunting arrows.

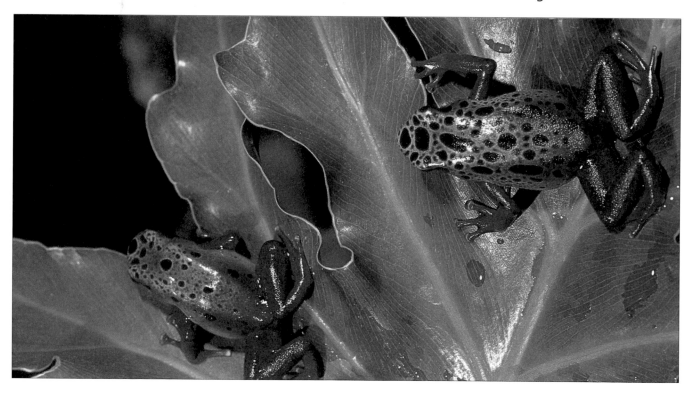

6

◁ **Country of volcanoes** Costa Rica has many volcanoes. Irazú is the highest, and 23 eruptions have been recorded in the past 276 years.

▽ **Dancing in the streets** Costa Ricans love to dance, and for many local festivities they dress in bright, traditional costumes.

The fact that Costa Rica joins two vastly different continents probably accounts for its most valuable resource—abundant and varied plants and animals. Although many forests have been cut down for coffee plantations and cattle, more than a quarter of the land is protected as national parks and reserves. Millions of tourists visit Costa Rica each year.

Costa Rica is Spanish for "rich coast." It was given this name in the 16th century by the first European explorers because they thought the land was full of gold. It was not. Instead, the Spanish settlers and the few Native Americans who survived the Spanish conquest worked the land. They developed into a closely knit community. After gaining independence from Spain in the early 19th century, Costa Rica became a rich country.

SAN JOSÉ

San José, the capital city, is set in a fertile valley surrounded by mountains that reach a height of 3,770 feet (1,150 m). About one-third of Costa Rica's population lives in the city and surrounding metropolitan areas.

Spanish traders founded San José in 1737. The central area is laid out in a grid pattern of streets and avenues. The streets, known as *calles*, run north to south. Avenues, or *avenidas*, run east to west. The main avenue is Avenida Central, which is known as Paseo Colón at its western end. Beyond Paseo Colón is La Sabana, a former airport that is now the largest park in the city. The American aviator Charles Lindbergh, famous for the first solo flight across the Atlantic Ocean, is said to have landed here once.

Most of the activity in the city takes place around the Plaza de Cultura on the southern side of the Avenida Central. Here, artists show their paintings and handicrafts, and all kinds of street entertainers amuse the crowds. One of the great attractions in the Plaza is the underground Gold Museum. It houses the finest collection of pre-Columbian gold molded and worked by the original inhabitants of the country.

Other well-known buildings in San José include the "Yellow House" (*Casa Amarilla*) or Ministry of Foreign Affairs. There is also the unusual "Metal House" (*Edifício Metálico*). This 19th-century relic was designed by the French engineer Alexandre Gustave Eiffel, who built the famous Eiffel Tower in Paris. The ornate National Theater, with its marble staircases, Venetian mirrors, and magnificent frescoes is most impressive. The theater first opened in 1897. Another great site is the famous Jade Museum, which houses the largest collection of American jade in the world.

◁ **The capital city** San José is set in a shallow valley. Long avenues run from the outskirts, passing through parks and tree-filled squares.

▷ **Street markets** Stalls loaded with fresh vegetables and fruits, such as these avocados, are part of everyday life in Costa Rican towns.

▽ **Traveling by bus** Many of Costa Rica's buses are old school buses brought from the United States. They travel routes all over the country and especially in San José.

CENTRAL VALLEY

Surrounding San José is an open patchwork of fields that stretch out across the flat plains and into the foothills of the mountains. Coffee plantations, fields of vegetables, corn, and other crops are found here.

The Central Valley area covers just six percent of the country, but including San José, it is home to seventy percent of the population. Costa Ricans today are mainly descended from Spanish and other European immigrants or are mixed-race *mestizos* born of Native American and Spanish parentage. The mestizos are known locally as *Ticos*, a nickname that probably comes from the common use of the Spanish word for "small," for example, *momentico* instead of *momento*.

The soil, altitude, and climate of the Central Valley are ideal for growing coffee. When coffee was first introduced into the highlands in the 1820s, it was recognized as having great economic potential. Production rose dramatically from 1834 to 1841—from 50,000 to 9 million pounds. But until the coming of the railroads in 1890, farmers had to use oxcarts to carry their coffee beans all the way to the coast for shipping abroad.

Today, in the small town of Sarchí not far from San José, you can still see the oxcarts being made. They are brightly painted and decorated with colorful flowers and other designs. Now only a few of the carts are used to carry coffee. They are seen mostly at fiestas or sold to tourists.

You can learn about the history of coffee in Costa Rica by visiting a coffee *finca* (plantation). Here, a guide will explain how in the 19th century people were given free land and seedlings and told to plant a certain number of coffee bushes. You will also learn how coffee is harvested today.

▽ **Drying coffee beans** Coffee beans are sun dried on special flat areas outside. Several times each day, workers turn the beans.

△ **Growing coffee**
Plantations of coffee bushes are a common sight among the cool, green hills of the region around San José.

◁ **Painted carts** Hand-painted carts, at one time, were part of the everyday village scene. Today the tradition continues at Sarchí.

VOLCANOES

The Central Valley is surrounded by high mountains and volcanoes, including Volcán Poás, Volcán Irazú, and Volcán Barva. Each volcano stands in its own national park, and few visitors leave the Central Valley without taking a trip to at least one.

Volcán Poás is close to Alajuela, Costa Rica's second-largest city. To see the volcano, you must be there early in the morning, before the crater is covered with clouds. Poás was last seriously active in 1910, but it still rumbles and occasionally spews out masses of lava. When exploring the park, you will find trails leading to waterfalls, steaming fumaroles (smoke holes), and a vivid green lake that has formed in an extinct crater. Trails also lead to a forest with trees whose growth has been strangely stunted by volcanic gases.

You can also make two other short trips from Alajuela. Go to the Butterfly Farm at La Guácima and visit Zoo-Ave. This sanctuary has a huge number of birds, including some of the area's most colorful toucans and parrots.

▽ **Wonders of nature** Wildlife and forests are two of Costa Rica's finest assets. Visitors who come specifically to see natural attractions, such as this butterfly, are called ecotourists.

Volcán Irazú, at 11,260 feet (3,432 m) high, dominates Cartago, Costa Rica's old capital city. The volcano erupted during U.S. President Kennedy's visit to Costa Rica in 1963. The city, including the huge cathedral, has been mostly rebuilt. An annual festival to honor the Virgin of Los Angeles is held here.

Northeast of Heredia, another main town in Costa Rica's Central Valley, is Volcán Barva in the Braulio Carrillo National Park. The forest is often covered in clouds, and it is easy to get lost. The best way to see the park is by Aerial Tram in an overhead cable car. The track runs close to the top of the forest so you can see the mammals, birds, and plants that live in the treetops.

◁ **Rich farmland** Land surrounding volcanoes is often good for agriculture. Almost all the land on the slopes of Irazú is used for farming.

▽ **Hillside city** Heredia is located on the hills of Barva. It lies on the Pan-American Highway, the major road running through Costa Rica.

 # CARIBBEAN COAST

For some spectacular sights, drive from San José to Limón Province and the Caribbean coast. The journey zigzags through the mountains and thick forest, crossing the Reventazón and Pacuare Rivers on the way. These are Costa Rica's best rivers for white-water rafting.

Limón Province occupies all of Costa Rica's Caribbean coast. It has more nature reserves than any other part of the country. In the north, the Barra del Colorado Refuge shares the border with Nicaragua. Only the great San Juan River divides the two countries. A strange inhabitant of this river is the bullshark. It swims from the Caribbean Sea upriver to Lake Nicaragua—apparently the only shark that is known to have adapted to fresh water.

South of Barra del Colorado is the very popular Tortuguero National Park. The park is huge and contains forests, mangrove swamps, and a long coastline. All sorts of birds, mammals, and insects can be found here. But the park gets its name from the Spanish word for "turtles," which nest and lay their eggs on its beaches every year.

In the southern part of the Limón Province there are four national parks and reserves. Chirripó and International Park of Friendship together comprise the region with the greatest variety of plant and animal life. Cahuita is on the coast and extends to a coral reef about 550 yards (500 m) offshore. This is a good place for snorkeling, but the reef is dying because of pollution and the build-up of sand in nearby rivers. Hitoy-Cerere is a biological reserve that is almost permanently drenched in rain. It is rich in forest life at different levels of altitude. Gandoca-Manzanillo features beaches with smooth slopes into calm waters. It has been set up to protect coral reefs and turtles.

▷ **Tropical plants** Heavy rains on the Caribbean coast produce rich rain forests with such beautiful plants as this young palm.

△ **Living on the coast** Costa Rica's Caribbean coastal area is far from the bustling capital. Here, home and daily life are of the simplest kind due to the lack of technology.

▽ **Lively street life** A street scene in Park Vargas located in the city of Puerto Limón. The park was planted with trees that were brought from India 150 years ago.

The largest town in Limón Province is Puerto Limón. It was the country's main port until Moín was built a few miles to the north. About one-third of the people are black or mixed-race mulatos. They are descendants of West Indians, mainly from Jamaica, who arrived in the 19th century to work on banana plantations. They spoke English, which has gradually been mixed with Spanish phrases, creating a local language, called *patois*.

Bananas grow especially well in the hot and humid lowlands. Because the banana plantations are practically cut off from the more-populated highland areas, they developed like small towns. They have their own schools, medical clinics, and churches, which are mainly Protestant. Railroads were needed to take the bananas to the coast. An American engineer named Minor Keith built the railroad. He later founded the North American-owned United Fruit Company.

Early in the 20th century, the banana plantations were destroyed by disease. Most closed down or were moved to the Pacific coast. In the new locations, plantation work was given first to white workers. The black people had to stay in the Caribbean lowlands, surviving as best they could. As a result, much of what you find in Limón is Afro-Caribbean. Spices of African origin are used in food with beans, coconut milk, and oil. Music is based on the African beat, with drums and other percussion instruments. Carnival in Puerto Limón is a noisy event with fireworks, brilliant costumes, floats, dancing, and much music.

Two small groups of Costa Rica's few surviving Native Americans, the Bribri and the Cabécar, live on a reservation in the Talamanca Mountains in the south. The people live in simple houses, wear mostly Western-style dress, and spend their time looking after their crops or making crafts.

▷ **Working on a banana plantation** Bananas are selected, washed, and dried before being packed for exporting.

△ **A religious procession**
On Good Friday, people carry a casket outside the Catholic church of the Holy Heart of Jesus (Parroquia Sagrado Corazon de Jesus) in Puerto Limón. The children are dressed as angels.

▷ **Street vendors** Many people make their living as street vendors in Costa Rica. Here, in Puerto Limón, the items on sale include clothes and table linen.

17

THE NORTHERN ZONE

Costa Rica's "Northern Zone" stretches from Limón Province in the east to Guanacaste Province in the west. To the south are the central highlands, and to the north are the San Juan River and the country of Nicaragua. The region differs in character from the rest of Costa Rica. The land is divided roughly into two plains—junglelike in the east and flat with pockets of rain forests, hills, and rivers in the west.

▽ **Seeing the sights from the river** River rafting is a good way for tourists to see Costa Rica's forests and wildlife.

The original inhabitants of this region were the Corobicí and the Guatusos peoples. Just a small group of these people have survived. The Spanish explored the San Juan River area, and eventually, together with other Europeans, settled in the region. Today it is cattle country. Small agricultural towns are linked by good roads, and it is easy to travel around the area. A good reason to visit the area is to see the Arenal Volcano.

▽ **Enjoying the waters** The Balneario Tabacón hot springs are fed by an underground thermal river from Arenal Volcano.

It is one of the world's most active volcanoes. Arenal is now the center of a tourist industry and has been declared a national park.

Near the volcano itself is Lake Arenal. Here, you can sail, windsurf, or go fishing. There are caves to explore and the scenery, with beautiful waterfalls, is spectacular. If you are feeling adventurous, follow one of the trails into the rain forest. But if you just want to relax, put on a swimsuit and enjoy the thermal springs of Balneario Tabacón. The water in some of the pools is around 72°F (40°C) all year round. People even make a daytime round trip from San José to take a dip in the springs.

△ **A surprise explosion** People thought that Arenal was a dormant, or inactive, volcano until it erupted on July 29, 1968, killing more than 60 people.

The Northern Zone of Costa Rica has several nature reserves. One of the most enterprising is Rara Avis in the east. Rara Avis includes a scientific research station dedicated to developing rain forest products, including orchids and palms, as crops. The aim is to persuade the local farmers that the rain forest itself can be as productive and profitable as cutting it down for cattle ranching would be.

19

LAND OF THE COWBOYS

Guanacaste lies to the west of Costa Rica's Northern Zone and incorporates the top two-thirds of the Nicoya Peninsula.

This area was almost not part of Costa Rica at all. In 1824, a vote was held to see if the area should be ruled by Nicaragua or Costa Rica. The people voted for Costa Rica, but only by a narrow margin. Traditionally, Guanacaste is the land of the cowboy, and much of the original forest has been cleared for cattle ranching. The best places to see the cowboys' skills of lassoing and riding bulls are at weekly village fairs, where rodeos are held. These events are often accompanied by brass bands and dancing.

Guanacaste was also the home of the Chorotegas people, who are considered to be the most advanced of the pre-Columbian (prior to 1500) civilizations. Some of their culture remains. In particular, a style of pottery with black-and-red designs is now made to sell to tourists. Corn-based snacks and drinks from that culture remain, also.

Most people travel to Guanacaste to visit its lovely beaches and national parks. The national parks contain many attractions.

▽ **Farming on the volcano** The volcano's slopes are extremely fertile. Here, farmers inspect onion fields on Volcano Miravelles.

△ **Keeping cows** The cattle industry developed in the 19th century and has been the most important part of the economy in the area.

◁ **Playa Conchal in Guanacaste Province**
This broad bay is protected by a rocky headland covered in scrub and forest. West of the headland there are many, many seashells, which is the reason for the name Playa Conchal (Place of Shells). Swimming is very good because you will find clear, blue waters.

In Barra Honda National Park, visitors can climb through the 40-foot (12-m)-deep caves that were discovered only about 30 years ago. Or they can scale the Rincón de la Vieja Volcano, set in its own park not far from Liberia, the provincial capital. This is a good park for horseback riding and hiking.

Parks in Guanacaste have a good range of Costa Rican wildlife. The parks provide migratory routes and shelter during the dry season, especially for insects. Scientists estimate that the parks have 2,250 plant species, 125 species of birds, 25 mammal species, and 1,800 species of insects.

CLOUD FOREST AND PACIFIC COAST

Travel a short distance south from Guanacaste to the cool, green heights of the Cordillera de Tilarán. Here, you will find Costa Rica's number-one tourist destination, the privately owned Monteverde Cloud Forest Reserve. Monteverde is in the Central Pacific region, which stretches south along the Pacific coast. The port of Puntarenas is on this coast. From here you can take a ferry across the Gulf of Nicoya to the southern Nicoya Peninsula, which is part of Puntarenas Province. From Puntarenas, take a boat to the uninhabited Tortuga Islands—a paradise of palm-fringed, white-sand beaches. Here, you can swim or snorkel in sheltered waters.

The Monteverde Reserve protects some of the only unspoiled cloud forest in Central America. It is home to more than 2,000 kinds

△ **The rich variety of rain forest life** The wealth of tropical blossoms in the Costa Rican forests attracts some of the tiniest birds in the world. This violet saberwing hummingbird is taking nectar from deep inside the flower.

▷ **Cloud Forests** Heavy clouds, such as these at the Monteverde Cloud Forest Reserve, form where the cool mountain air meets warm humid air.

22

of plants. More than 100 mammal species and some 500 species of butterflies make their homes here. So, too, do more than 400 species of birds, including the rare quetzal. This reserve was started by a group of Quakers from the state of Alabama. The religious sect settled in the isolated area in 1951, where they built homes, a school, and a meeting house. They also developed a successful dairy industry,

which supplies milk products to stores all over Costa Rica. Not far from Monteverde is the "Children's Eternal Rain Forest" funded by schoolchildren worldwide.

One of Costa Rica's prettiest and most popular beaches is Montezuma in southern Nicoya. South of Puntarenas is the equally popular Manuel Antonio National Park with beautiful, well-protected beaches, mangrove swamps, and tropical forests. There are other beaches outside the park and plenty to do. Whether your choice of activity is hiking, horseback riding, swimming, white-water rafting, fishing, cruising, or surfing, it will be against a backdrop of spectacular scenery.

△ **Exploring the forest** A group of tourists in the Monteverde Cloud Forest Reserve stops to use a spotting telescope to identify birds.

Continuing farther south from Manuel Antonio National Park, you enter Costa Rica's "Southern Zone." This is a large area that covers much of the southwest. Although the roads have recently been paved, this part of the coast is still largely undeveloped. However, this will probably not be true for much longer. Small, pretty fishing villages like Dominical will almost certainly soon become tourist centers. For the present, you can enjoy the white-sand, palm-fringed, quiet beaches and beautiful Pacific sunsets. For another treat, try the little-visited National Ballenas Park; it is named for the humpback (a type of "baleen") whales that occasionally are seen there.

As you approach the Golfito area and the Osa Peninsula, you are entering the land once inhabited by the pre-Columbian Diquis civilization. Little is known about the Diquis people, but they left behind some mysterious structures. Huge, perfectly shaped, stone spheres, up to 6 feet (2 m) in diameter, are dotted here and there in this region, but no one knows why.

Golfito, a former banana port, sits among magnificent scenery and is the only town here of any size. Between it and the Osa Peninsula is a strikingly beautiful body of water—*Golfo Dulce*, or Sweet Gulf.

More than 300 miles (500 km) offshore lies Coco Island. Once a haven for pirates, it is now a bird reserve and a popular place to scuba dive. For most people, a visit to the Corcovado National Park on the Osa Peninsula is challenge enough. Be prepared for hot, rainy days, and tough hikes through impressive forests of huge trees, covered in *lianas* (climbing vines). Watch out for herds of peccaries—they can stampede—snakes, and crocodiles. However, it is more likely you will see harmless agoutis, coatis, the minklike tayras, and many birds. If you are very lucky, you will also see the margay, or ocelot, a member of the cat family.

▽ **Looking for gold** Prospecting and panning for gold still draws men and women to the rivers in the Osa Peninsula.

◁ Living in the trees
Tamanduas—a type of anteater—tend to live in the trees where they feed on ants and termites.

▽ Black sands Some of the beaches of the Golfo Dulce in the far southwest of the country are composed of black, volcanic ash.

CORDILLERA DE TALAMANCA

Not far from the town of Golfito you can pick up the Inter-American Highway. This road runs the length of Costa Rica and takes you across the Cordillera de Talamanca, back to San José. The highway leads north through a coffee-growing zone before coming to a small reservation where a few families of Boruca Native Americans live.

The Boruca people have simple homes of wood and thatch (straw and mud), grow their own crops, and weave cloth on homemade looms, which they sell to the occasional tourist. The Boruca are best known for the "fiesta of the devils." This event takes place over three days at the New Year. Here, they re-enact the story of the Spanish conquest with a bull (the Spaniards) against the "devils" (the local people). Today, unlike the historical event, the fiesta is peaceful and fun, and the "devils" win!

Farther north is the modern town of San Isidro de el General. The town sits at about 2,300 feet (702 m) above sea level, in the highly cultivated Valle de el General. To the northeast of San Isidro is the Chirripó National Park and Chirripó Grande, Costa Rica's highest peak at 12,530 feet (3,819 m). For those able to climb the mountain, it is a chance to see glaciers, glacier lakes, and grasses of the high-level *páramo*, or plateau.

From San Isidro the road climbs to almost 11,500 feet (3,500 m) over the "Hill of Death" pass. The view is spectacular, but falling rocks, landslides, fog, and very heavy traffic all make this a dangerous road. The road descends into the Central Valley, and from there it is a short drive back to San José, where your started your tour of Costa Rica.

◁ **Native Americans** This Boruca woman lives on a reservation in a traditional-style house.

▷ **A cash crop** Pineapples are one of the country's most-successful crops. The fruit grows near the ground within a tight circle of very spiky leaves. Today, modern machinery is used for the harvest.

▽ **Growing plants for ropes** Sisal is a plant of Central America, and for centuries fibers from its leaves have been used to make ropes and rugs. Now it is grown commercially and the fibers are exported.

COSTA RICA FACTS AND FIGURES

People

Most Costa Ricans are descended from Europeans who arrived in the 19th century. The settlers came mainly from Spain, but also from Britain, Germany, and France.

Mestizos, or people of Spanish and Native American blood, have increased in number, but still represent less than 10 percent of the population. The smallest group is the original Native Americans, who probably number fewer than 10,000.

Trade and Industry

Manufacturing in Costa Rica is based largely on agricultural crops. Factories produce canned foods, such as fruit, meat, vegetables, and drinks, particularly instant coffee. There is also a leather industry. Other manufactured goods include textiles, banana paper, chemicals, and plastics.

Costa Rica has some minerals, including bauxite and manganese, as well as some gold, silver, and iron. Hydroelectric dams provide most of the country's energy.

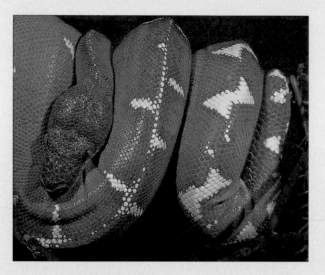

△ **Emerald Tree Boa** This snake's coloring is good camouflage for life in the forest. Tree boas coil themselves in a series of loops with their head resting on the coils.

Tourism is the country's most important and profitable industry. Millions of ecotourists visit the country's many national parks and reserves, where many plants and animals are protected. Other tourists come to swim in the clear, blue waters or to visit some of the active volcanoes.

Fishing

Fish is an important source of food in the coastal areas and includes red snapper, sea bass, and lobster. Costa Rica has a growing fishing industry, mainly shrimp, sardines, and tuna.

Farming

Agriculture produces more than 60 percent of Costa Rica's foreign earnings and employs over 25 percent of the country's workforce. The two principal crops are coffee and bananas. Other crops grown for the domestic market include rice, beans, and maize. Sugarcane is another major product, and it is used in part for making fuel from the unused fiber, or bagasse, left after milling.

Forestry

Costa Rica has good timber resources. Because of the large-scale clearance of forests in recent years, the government has limited this industry at present. Replanting programs are being planned.

Food

The two most basic foods are beans and rice, and they are generally eaten with meat or fish. Beans, rice, meat with plantains (a type of banana), and cabbage make up *casado*. In the highlands, *gallo pinto*, meaning "painted rooster," is the nearest thing to a national dish. It consists of black or red beans, rice, onions, peppers, and seasonings. Among the most popular fish dishes is *ceviche*, made of raw fish marinated in lemon or lime juice. In the Caribbean region, fish is mixed with coconut milk and different herbs and spices to give a more West Indian flavor to the food. Dishes in the area of Guanacaste are largely based on corn, such as *tortillas* filled with chicken, meat, or cheese. They are eaten as snacks and main dishes. *Tamales* are one of the most important festival foods. They are like pancakes made of corn dough, filled, and cooked in banana leaves.

△ **Local cooking relies on simple ingredients** Boiled green bananas soon turn a delicious golden brown when fried in hot oil.

Schools

In 1869, Costa Rica became one of the first Latin American countries to make education compulsory and free for all children. Today, 95 percent of the population can read and write. Children go to school from the ages of six to fifteen, with the first six years at primary level. After three years at secondary level, the students who pass exams can choose to go on to a university. There are six universities in Costa Rica, with a wide range of courses that include academic and technical subjects, such as law, medicine, sociology, fine arts, and journalism.

The Media

Major newspapers include *La Nación*, which has the largest distribution— more than 100,000. Others include *La República*, *La Prensa Libre*, and *Esta Semana*, which has good in-depth articles. There is no censorship of the press, and reporting covers all topics, though most Costa Rican newspapers feature sports, especially soccer. There are two English-language papers, the *Tico Times*, and the all-color *Costa Rica Today*, which is intended for tourists. Costa Rica has more than 50 radio stations, a government-owned television channel, and several commercial TV stations. Programs range from news, documentaries, and sports coverage to "soap operas" and imported films.

Art

Some of Costa Rica's finest works are jade and gold artifacts made by the pre-Columbian peoples. The best-known folk art is the painted oxcart, once used for transporting coffee beans. Costa Rica's leading engraver and painter of the 20th century, Francisco Amighetti Ruiz, was born in 1907.

Music

The most popular modern instruments are the guitar and xylophone-like *marimba*. Modern music includes Latin rhythms, rock, and dance music such as the *salsa* and *cumbia*. Costa Rica's National Symphony Orchestra tours the country and also tours and plays internationally.

Religion

Roman Catholicism is the official religion, and about 80 percent of Costa Ricans are Catholic. In Limón Province, the black population is traditionally Protestant. Today, Evangelical Protestantism is becoming popular in the rest of the country through groups such as the Assemblies of God and Jehovah's Witnesses.

Festival and Holidays

Many national holidays are religious.
January 1 **New Year's Day**
March 19 **St. Joseph's Day** Honors the patron saint of San José
April 11 **Juan Santamaría Day** Commemorates the national hero of the Battle of Rivas in 1856

△ **Riding on horseback** Horseback riding is part of the daily life. These riders from Guanacaste Province in the northwest are on their way to a local festival.

May 1 **Labor Day**
August 2 **Virgin of Los Angeles Day** (patron saint of Costa Rica)
August 15 **Assumption Day and Mother's Day**
September 15 **Independence Day** Celebrating Costa Rica's independence from Spain in 1821
October 12 **Columbus Day**
November 2 **All Soul's Day**
December 25 **Christmas Day**

Sports

The most popular game in Costa Rica is *fútbol*, or soccer. Other sports include cycling, basketball, volleyball, baseball, tennis, and, to a limited extent, golf and polo. Almost every kind of watersport is possible in Costa Rica, with parts of the coast particularly good for surfing. Rivers, like the Reventazón, are excellent sites for white-water rafting. Horseback riding is also very popular. Costa Rica's most-famous athlete is Claudia Poll, the World and Olympic 400- and 800-meter freestyle swimmer.

Plants and Animals

In the national parks and reserves, there are many types of forest, with orchids, bromeliads, lianas, and other plants. Costa Rica has some 850 species of birds. Mammals include many members of the cat family—jaguar, jaguarundi, ocelot, and margay. There are also rodents, anteaters, sloths, and many species of monkeys. At least five species of turtles nest on the Costa Rican shores. In addition, whales and dolphins are protected, while fish, especially big game fish such as sharks, are abundant offshore. There are thousands of insect species and many kinds of spiders.

HISTORY

Costa Rica's first inhabitants lived by hunting wild animals and fishing. Christopher Columbus landed here in 1502, but the first capital city, Cartago, was not founded until 1564.

The early European settlers who brought in cattle, pigs, and horses, found no mineral wealth. During 300 years of colonial rule, the Spanish settlers and Native Americans were isolated from the rest of America. They developed into a closely knit community.

In 1821, Costa Rica became completely independent from Spain. Between 1856 and 1858, there was civil war, when William Walker, a North American, tried to take over the country but did not succeed.

Eventually, in 1890, José Joaquin Rodriquez became the first president under the constitution. However, political unrest continued. In 1940 a new president, Rafael Angel Calderon, introduced social and labor reforms to help the poor people. However, Calderon then turned to the Communists for support, and this led to another civil war and the emergence of a new leader, "Don Pepe" Figueres.

Don Pepe dominated Costa Rican politics for years. When he retired in 1974, the country was in debt. Since then, presidents have improved the economy. Oscar Arias Sanchez, who was president from 1986 to 1990, won the Nobel Peace Prize for bringing five Central American countries to sign a peace plan.

LANGUAGE

Spanish is the official language of Costa Rica and is spoken and understood in every part of the country. Many people also speak English, partly as a result of immigration from Europe and North America. Most young people speak Spanish. Many Native American languages have disappeared, though Bribri and Cabécar are still spoken by the local inhabitants of the Talamanca Mountains. An effort is being made to save these languages by using them on local radio programs.

Useful words and phrases

English	Spanish
One	*Uno*
Two	*Dos*
Three	*Tres*
Four	*Cuatro*
Five	*Cinco*
Six	*Seis*
Seven	*Siete*
Eight	*Ocho*
Nine	*Nueve*
Ten	*Diez*
Sunday	*Domingo*
Monday	*Lunes*
Tuesday	*Martes*
Wednesday	*Miércoles*

Useful words and phrases

English	Spanish
Thursday	*Jueves*
Friday	*Viernes*
Saturday	*Sábado*
Hello	*Hola*
Good-bye	*Adiós*
Good morning	*Buenos días*
Good afternoon	*Buenas tardes*
Good night	*Buenas noches*
Please	*Por favor*
Thank you	*Gracias*
Yes/No	*Sí/No*
How are you?	*¿Cómo está?*
Can you speak English?	*¿Habla usted Inglés?*

INDEX

Acknowledgments
Book created for Highlights for Children, Inc. by Bender Richardson White.
Editors: Belinda Weber and Lionel Bender
Designer: Mike Pilley, Pelican Graphics
Art Editor: Ben White
Picture Researcher: Cathy Stastny and Daniela Marceddu
Production: Kim Richardson

Maps produced by Oxford Cartographers, England.
Banknotes from Thomas Cook Currency Services.
Stamps from Stanley Gibbons.

Editorial Consultant: Andrew Gutelle
Guide to Costa Rica is approved by the Costa Rica Tourist Office, London
Costa Rica Consultant: Marilyn E. de Sauter
Managing Editor, Highlights New Products: Margie Hayes Richmond

Picture credits
SAP = South American Photos, OSF = Oxford Scientific Films, COR = CORBIS, UK, EU = Eye Ubiquitous, JDTP = James Davis Travel Photography. t = top, b = bottom, l = left, r = right.
Cover: Z/Everts. 6 OSF/John Netherton. 7t: JDTP. 7b: COR/Kit Kittle. 8: JDTP. 9t: SAP/Tony Morrison. 9b: COR/The Purcell Team. 10: SAP/Robert Francis. 11t: Still Pictures/Chris Cablicott. 11b: Robert Harding/Jeff Greenberg. 12: OSF/Michael Fodgen. 13t: Costa Rica Tourist Office. 13b and 14-15: SAP/Robert Francis. 15t and 15b: COR/Martin Rogers. 16: EU/D. Forman. 17t and 17b: COR/Martin Rogers. 18l: Robert Harding/Nik Wheeler. 18r: SAP/Robert Francis. 19: SAP/Jevan Berrange. 20: SAP/Robert Francis. 21t: SAP/Jevan Berrange. 21b: JDTP. 22 and 22-23: OSF/Michael Fogden. 23: SAP/Robert Francis. 24: SAP/Jevan Berrange. 25t: OSF/Michael Fogdon. 25b: Still Pictures/Chris Caldicott. 26: Life File/Flora Torrance. 27t and 27b: SAP/Jevan Berrange. 28: OSF/Zig Leszczynski. 29: DAS Photos/David Simson. 30: COR/ Martin Rogers. Illustration on page 1 by Tom Powers.